T0086970

Cecilia McDowall

Music of the Stars

for SATB and piano or strings and percussion

vocal score

OXFORD
UNIVERSITY PRESS

OXFORD
UNIVERSITY PRESS

Great Clarendon Street, Oxford OX2 6DP,
United Kingdom

Oxford University Press is a department of the University of Oxford.
It furthers the University's objective of excellence in research, scholarship,
and education by publishing worldwide. Oxford is a registered trade mark of
Oxford University Press in the UK and in certain other countries

This work © Oxford University Press 2023

Cecilia McDowall has asserted her right under the Copyright, Designs
and Patents Act, 1988, to be identified as the Composer of this Work

First published 2023

Impression: 1

All rights reserved. No part of this publication may be reproduced,
stored in a retrieval system, or transmitted, in any form or by any means,
without the prior permission in writing of Oxford University Press

Permission to perform this work in public (except in the course of divine worship)
should normally be obtained from a local performing right licensing organization,
unless the owner or the occupier of the premises being used already holds a licence
from such an organization. Likewise, permission to make and exploit a recording of this work
should be obtained from a local mechanical copyright licensing organization

Enquiries concerning reproduction outside the scope of the above
should be directed to the Music Rights Department, Oxford University Press,
at music.permissions.uk@oup.com or at the address above

ISBN 978–0–19–356428–2

Music origination by Anna Williams
Text origination by Katie Johnston

Printed in Great Britain on acid-free paper by
Halstan & Co. Ltd, Amersham, Bucks.

Contents

Composer's note iv
Texts v

1. Music of the Stars 1
2. The hardest thing 12
3. The Gift to Sing 24

Duration: 13 minutes

Instrumentation

percussion—1 player (vibraphone, glockenspiel, suspended cymbal)
strings

Full scores and instrumental parts are available on hire/rental.

If required, the work may also be accompanied by piano, playing from the vocal score.

Composer's note

Music of the Stars was commissioned by long-time Chamber Singers of Iowa City member, James Petersen, and his spouse, David McCartney, to celebrate the Chamber Singers' fiftieth season.

James and David suggested a commission which could celebrate the power of music in these difficult times. I was most touched to be offered such a rewarding opportunity. Finding just the right text to set is such an interesting process and I felt this one was particularly engaging. In recognition of the racial issues which face us every day, the commissioners and music director, David Puderbaugh, offered texts written by people of colour: James Weldon Johnson and Kenyan-born Brian Odongo. The latter text was discovered by another CSIC singer, Elaine Reding. To continue the theme of music, singing, and the stars, I discovered an absorbing explanation of 'light' and how we perceive it by the American astrophysicist Neil deGrasse Tyson. He is an outstanding science communicator and I found myself drawn to and fascinated by his planetary postings, which have a clarity I had not encountered before.

The atmospheric text of the first movement, 'Music of the Stars', evokes 'dark night clouds', illuminated by ancient, radiant stars as they watch over mortals' adventures below; the 'music of the stars' sings to 'seafarers, wayfarers, and soldiers'. There is a gentle, almost mesmerizing pace to the poem which I hope is reflected in the music. I wove just a small part of a Ukrainian folksong into this movement—*In the garden flowers are growing, Boys will quarrel where I'm going*—as it just seemed impossible to ignore the unfolding horror in Ukraine. I would be mortified if this seemed a posturing gesture but as I was writing I found it hard not to be affected by these shocking events and to feel, at the same time, utterly powerless as a witness.

In the text of the second, up-tempo movement, 'The hardest thing', Tyson explores the concept of how we analyse colour. Certainly, when reading Tyson's explanation of how the universe is studied, one begins to sense what an extraordinarily complex science astrophysics is. Setting prose to music needs a different approach, I feel, and I aimed to bring a more conversational style to the word setting, sometimes repeating the little phrase endings, to give a little more emphasis.

The poem 'The Gift to Sing' will be so familiar to many. I found this a wonderful poem to set; there is something so quietly confident, so intimate and ultimately joyful about it. Each verse ends with a solution to the day's challenges—'I softly sing'; 'And sing, and sing'; 'And I can sing'. These heart-warming words bring an affirmation of what the power of singing can do for us all in times of difficulty. The text speaks to us all in these most exacting times. How glorious it is, at last, to sing again. I do hope this work brings a response to the times in which we now live.

This note may be reproduced as required for programme notes.

Texts

1. Music of the Stars

The dark night clouds are starlit
As though to mock the moon
That arises at each twilight
To take the mantle from the sun
All united in an assignment
To light the dark auditorium below
The radiant stars gloriously move
Age to age whispering its adventures
It's the music of the stars
Singing the past, present and future
Singing a past heard in legends
Singing a present felt by all men
Singing a future obscure to mortals
It's the music of the stars.

The inaudible lyrics of the stars
That need neither lute nor lyre
To arouse the heart with its ancient rhyme
That chime that is older than any note
Like a spell enchants the audience.

Its melody wanes towards daybreak
Like a script come to a timely end
Its rhythm diminishes
Like the beats fleeting from dawn
Its harmony disaccords
Like harpers' strings breaking,
Singing a ballad to seafarers
Singing a hymn to wayfarers
Singing an anthem to soldiers
It's the music of the stars.

Brian Odongo (b. 1994), adap.
© Brian Odongo. Used by permission.

**Ukrainian folksong*

**In the garden flowers are growing,*
Boys will quarrel where I'm going.

2. The hardest thing

The hardest thing, I think, by far, is how we analyze spectra—light broken up into its component colors. It's so abstract, so removed from the actual object we are studying. See, chemists study chemicals in the lab. See, biologists study life on Earth. But astrophysicists can't grab a piece of a galaxy and put it in a laboratory. We have to study a picture of the thing, and then analyze the light that comes from it. Nearly everything we know about the machinery of our universe comes to us through the analysis of light. It's all just light—and ninety-nine percent of it happens to be invisible to the naked eye.

Neil deGrasse Tyson (b. 1958), adap.
© Neil D Tyson. Used by permission. All rights reserved.

3. The Gift to Sing

Sometimes the mist overhangs my path,
And blackening clouds about me cling;
But, oh, I have a magic way
To turn the gloom to cheerful day—
    I softly sing.

And if the way grows darker still,
Shadowed by Sorrow's somber wing,
With glad defiance in my throat,
I pierce the darkness with a note,
    And sing, and sing.

I brood not over the broken past,
Nor dread whatever time may bring;
No nights are dark, no days are long,
While in my heart there swells a song,
    And I can sing.

James Weldon Johnson (1871–1938)

Commissioned for the Chamber Singers of Iowa City, David Puderbaugh, Music Director, by James Petersen and David McCartney on the occasion of the choir's 50th anniversary season

Music of the Stars

CECILIA McDOWALL

1. Music of the Stars

Brian Odongo (b. 1994), adap.

Music © Oxford University Press 2023. Text © Brian Odongo. Used by permission.

Printed in Great Britain

OXFORD UNIVERSITY PRESS, MUSIC DEPARTMENT, GREAT CLARENDON STREET, OXFORD OX2 6DP

The Moral Rights of the Composer have been asserted. Photocopying this copyright material is ILLEGAL.

14
mp
moon
mp
moon
mf espress.
mp
That a - ri - ses at each twi - light To take the man-tle from the sun
mf espress.
mp
That a - ri - ses at each twi - light To take the man-tle from the sun
mp

21
mf
mp
All u - nit - ed in an as - sign - ment To light, mm
mf
mp
All u - nit - ed in an as - sign - ment To light, mm
mf
mp
All u - nit - ed in an as - sign - ment To light, mm
mf
f
All u - nit - ed in an as - sign - ment To light, to light the dark au - di -
mf
f

27
B
mf
mp
mp
dolce
light the dark,
The
light the dark,
The
light the dark,
- to - ri-um be - low
B
mf
mp
34
mf
ra - di-ant stars glo-rious-ly move Age to age, the stars move,
ra - di-ant stars glo-rious-ly move Age to age, the stars move,
Age to age, the stars, age to age
Age to age, the stars, age to age

40
mp
p
mp
whis - per-ing,
mp
p
mp
whis-per-ing,
mp
p
whis-per-ing its ad-ven- tures, its ad-ven - tures, whis-per - ing, whis-per-ing,
mp
p
whis-per-ing its ad-ven- tures, its ad-ven - tures, whis-per- ing, whis-per-ing, whis-per - ing,
mp
p
46
p
mp
mf
whis-per - ing, It's the mu - sic of the stars, the mu - sic
p
mp
mf
It's the mu - sic of the stars, the mu - sic
mp
p
mp
mf
whis-per - ing, It's the mu - sic of the stars, the mu - sic
mp
p
mf
the mu - sic
mp
p
mp
mf

C
53
f
mf
of the stars
of the stars
Sing-
of the stars
Sing - ing a past heard in le - gends,
of the stars
Sing - ing the past, pres-ent and fu-ture, sing - - ing,
C
60
Sing - ing a fu-ture ob - scure to mor-tals, ah It's the mu - sic of the stars,
- ing a pres-ent felt by all men, sing - ing, ah It's the mu - sic of the stars,
sing - - ing, sing - ing, ah It's the mu - sic of the stars,
sing - - - ing, sing - ing, ah It's the mu - sic of the stars,

*Ukrainian folksong

81
mf
To a-rouse the heart with its an - cient rhyme That chime that is
mf
To a-rouse the heart with its an - cient rhyme That chime that is
mf
Boys will quar - rel where I'm go - ing.
mf
Boys will quar - rel where I'm go - ing.
mf
88
f
mf
E
old - er than a - ny note
f
mf
old - er than a - ny note
f
Like a spell en - chants the au-di-ence.
f
Like a spell en - chants the au-di-ence.
E
f
mf

95
mf
Its me-lo-dy wanes to-wards day-break Like a
mf
Its me-lo-dy wanes to-wards day-break Like a
f
mf
102
mp
script, a script,
mp
script, a script,
mf
mp
Like a script, like a script come to a time - ly end
mf
mp
Like a script, like a script come to a time - ly end

109
mf
mp
Its rhy - thm di - mi-nish-es Like the beats fleet-ing from dawn, mm
Its rhy - thm di - mi-nish-es Like the beats fleet-ing from dawn, mm
Its rhy - thm di - mi-nish-es Like the beats fleet-ing from dawn, mm
Its rhy - thm di - mi-nish-es Like the beats fleet-ing from dawn, like the beats fleet - ing,
f
116
from dawn
from dawn
from dawn
fleet-ing from dawn
F
mp
espress.
Its
Its
F

123
f
mf
har-mo-ny dis - ac - cords Like harp - - - ers' strings
f
mf
har-mo-ny dis - ac - cords Like harp - - - ers' strings
mf
f
Like harp-ers' strings break-ing, strings break-ing,
mf
f
Like harp-ers' strings break-ing, strings break-ing,
f
mf
130
mp
mf
break-ing, Sing-
mp
mf
break-ing, Sing - ing an an-them to
mf
Sing - ing a hymn to way - far - ers, sing - -
mf
Sing - ing a bal-lad to sea - far-ers, sing - - ing, sing -

136
f mp mf
- ing an an-them to sol - diers, sing - ing, ah It's the mu - sic of the stars,
f mp mf
sol - diers, sing - ing, ah It's the mu - sic of the stars,
f mp mf
- ing, sing - ing, ah It's the mu - sic of the stars,
f mp mf
- - ing, sing - ing, ah It's the mu - sic of the stars,
f mp mf
143
f
ritardando
mf
it's the mu - sic of the stars.
f
mf
it's the mu - sic of the stars.
f
mf
it's the mu - sic of the stars.
f
mf
it's the mu - sic of the stars.
ritardando
f
mf

2. *The hardest thing*

Neil deGrasse Tyson (b. 1958), adap.

Music © Oxford University Press 2023. Text © Neil D Tyson. Used by permission. All rights reserved. Photocopying this copyright material is ILLEGAL.

7
mf mp mf mp
the hard - est thing, I think, by far, by far,
the hard - est thing, I think, by far, by far,
the hard - est thing, I think, by far, the hard - est thing, by far,
the hard - est thing, I think, by far, the hard - est thing, by far,
11
mf mp
is how we a - na - lyze, how we a - na - lyze spec -
is how we a - na - lyze, how we a - na - lyze spec -
is how we a - na - lyze spec -
is how we a - na - lyze spec -
f mf mp

15
- tra, spec - - tra— light bro - ken, bro-ken,
- - tra, spec - tra— light bro - ken, bro-ken,
- tra, spec - - tra— light bro-ken,
- - tra, spec - tra— light bro-ken,
19
bro - - ken up in - to its com-po - nent co - lors, com-po - nent co - - lors.
bro - - ken up in - to its com-po - nent co - lors, com-po - nent co - - lors.
bro - - ken up in - to its co - lors, com - po - nent co - lors.
bro - - ken up in - to its co - lors, com - po - nent co - lors.

23
A
mp
mf intense
It's so ab-stract, so ab-stract, so re-
mp
mf intense
It's so ab-stract, so ab-stract, so re-
mp
mf intense
It's so ab-stract, so ab-stract, so re-
mp
mf intense
It's so ab-stract, so ab-stract, so re-
A
mp
mf
27
mp dolce
-moved, re-moved from the ac-tual ob-ject we are stu-dying, so re-
mp dolce
-moved, re-moved from the ac-tual ob-ject we are stu-dying, so re-
mp dolce
-moved, re-moved from the ac-tual ob-ject we are stu-dying, so re-
mp dolce
-moved, re-moved from the ac-tual ob-ject we are stu-dying, so re-
mp dolce

31
mf
mp
- moved, it's so ab - stract.
- moved, it's so ab - stract.
- moved, it's so ab - stract.
- moved, it's so ab - stract.
B
35
mp
p
See, see, che-mists, che - mists stu-dy
See, see, che-mists, che - mists stu-dy
See, see,
See, see,
B

39
mf mp mf mp p mp p
che-mi-cals in the lab. See, see,
mf mp mf mp p mp p
che-mi-cals in the lab. See, see,
mf mp mf mp p mp
see, lab. See, see,
mf mp mf mp p mp
see, lab. See, see,
mf mp
43
mf f mf mp
bi - o - lo-gists stu - dy, stu - dy life on Earth.
mf f mf mp
bi - o - lo-gists stu - dy, stu - dy life on Earth.
mf f mf mp
bi - o - lo-gists stu - dy, stu - dy life on Earth.
mf f mf mp
bi - o - lo-gists stu - dy, stu - dy life on Earth.
mf f mf

46
C
mf leggiero
But
mf leggiero
But
mf leggiero
But
mf leggiero
But
C
f mf
f mf
50
mf mf f
as - tro-phy-si-cists, as - tro-, as - tro-phy-si-cists can't grab a piece of a
as - tro-phy-si-cists, as - tro-, as - tro-phy-si-cists can't grab a piece of a
as - tro-phy-si-cists, as - tro-, as - tro-phy-si-cists can't grab a piece of a
as - tro-phy-si-cists, as - tro-, as - tro-phy-si-cists can't grab a piece of a
f

53
mf
ga - la - xy,
mf
ga - la - xy,
mf
ga - la - xy and put it in a, put it in a la -
mf
ga - la - xy and put it in a, put it in a la -
mf mp mf mp mf mp
56
mf f mf
ah
mf f mf
ah We have to stu - dy, stu-dy a
f mf
- bo - ra - t'ry. We have to stu - dy, stu-dy a
f mf
- bo - ra - t'ry. We have to stu - dy, stu-dy a
f mf mp mf

59
mf
f
and then a - na - lyze the
pic - ture of the, of the thing, and then a - na - lyze the
pic - ture of the, of the thing, then a - na - lyze the
pic - ture of the, of the thing, then a - na - lyze the
mp
62
light that comes, the light that comes from it.
light that comes, the light that comes from it.
light that comes, that comes from it, comes from it.
light that comes, that comes from it, comes from it.

D
65
mp
mf
mp
Near - ly ev - - - 'ry - thing, ev - 'ry-
mp
mf
mp
Near - ly ev - - - 'ry - thing, ev - 'ry-
mp
p
mp
Near - ly ev - 'ry - thing, ev - 'ry-
mp
p
mp
Near - ly ev - 'ry - thing, ev - 'ry-
D
mp
mf
68
mf
mp
-thing we know a - bout the ma-chi - ne - ry, we know,
mf
mp
-thing we know a - bout the ma-chi - ne - ry, we know,
mf
mp
-thing we know a - bout the ma-chi - ne - ry of our u - ni - verse, we know,
mf
mp
-thing we know a - bout the ma-chi - ne - ry of our u - ni - verse, we know,
mp
mf

71
mf
comes to us through the a - na - ly - sis of light, a - na - ly - sis of
mf
comes to us through the a - na - ly - sis of light, a - na - ly - sis of
mf
a - na - ly - sis of light.
mf
a - na - ly - sis of light.
f
mf
74
mp
f
light. It's all just light— and nine - ty-nine per-cent of it hap-pens to
mp
f
light. It's all just light— and nine - ty-nine per-cent of it hap-pens to
mp
f
It's all just light— and nine - ty-nine per-cent of it hap-pens to
mp
f
It's all just light— and nine - ty-nine per-cent of it hap-pens to
mp
f

poco rit. al fine
78
be in-vi-si-ble to the na - - - ked eye, to the
be in-vi-si-ble to the na - - - ked eye, to the
be in-vi-si-ble to the na - - - ked eye, to the
be in-vi-si-ble to the na - - - ked eye, to the
poco rit. al fine
81
mp
na-ked eye, the eye.
na-ked eye, the eye.
na-ked eye, the eye, na-ked eye.
(opt. div.)
na-ked eye, the eye, na-ked eye.
mp

3. *The Gift to Sing*

James Weldon Johnson (1871–1938)

© Oxford University Press 2023. Photocopying this copyright material is ILLEGAL.

13
mf
mp
mf
o'er-hangs my path, my path, ah o'er-hangs my
o'er-hangs my path, my path, ah o'er-hangs my
mist, some - times, some-times the mist o'er-hangs my path,
mist, some - times, some-times the mist o'er-hangs my path,
19
B
path,
And
path, my path,
my path,
my path,
f
3

24
f
mf
black-'ning clouds a-bout me cling, clouds, and
f
black - 'ning clouds a-bout me cling,
f
black-'ning clouds a-bout me cling, clouds,
f
black - 'ning clouds a-bout me cling,
3
f
29
p
mp
black-'ning clouds, clouds; But, oh, I
mf
p
mp
a - bout me cling, clouds; But, oh, I
mf
p
mp
and black-'ning clouds; But, oh, I
mf
p
mp
a-bout me cling; But, oh, I
p
mp

C
35
mf mp mf f
have a ma - gic way, a way To turn the gloom, to turn the
have a ma - gic way, a way To turn the gloom, to turn the
have a ma - gic way, a way To turn the gloom, to turn the
have a ma - gic way, a way To turn the gloom, to turn the
C
41
gloom to cheer - ful, cheer - ful day I soft - ly sing,
gloom to cheer - ful, cheer - ful day I soft - ly sing,
gloom to cheer - ful, cheer - ful day I soft - ly sing,
gloom, the gloom to cheer - ful day I soft - ly

47
D
p
sing.
sing.
sing.
sing, sing.
mp
And if the
And if the
D
p mp
53
mf
mp
ah
ah
And if the way
grows dark - er
way
grows dark - er still,
dark - er still, grows
way
grows dark - er
still,
dark - er still, grows

59
E
mf
mp
still,
Sha - dowed by Sor-row's
still,
Sha - dowed by
dark - er still,
Sha - dowed by Sor-row's
dark - er still,
Sha - dowed by
E
f
65
som - ber wing, Sor - row's,
With
som - ber wing,
With
som - ber wing, Sor - row's,
With
som - ber wing,
With

70
mf
mp
mf
glad de - fi - ance in my throat, de - fi - ance in my throat, I
glad de - fi - ance in my throat, de - fi - ance in my throat, I
glad de - fi - ance in my throat, de - fi - ance in my throat, I
glad de - fi - ance in my throat, de - fi - ance in my throat, I
F
75
f
mf
pierce the dark - ness, I pierce the dark - ness with a note,
pierce the dark - ness, I pierce the dark - ness with a note,
pierce the dark - ness, I pierce the dark - ness with a note,
pierce the dark - ness, I pierce the dark - ness with a
F

80
p mp mf
And sing, and sing, and sing, sing, and
And sing, and sing, and sing, sing, and
And sing, and sing, and sing, sing, and
mp mp mf
note, a note, And sing, and sing, and
p mf
85
mp p
sing, I soft - ly sing, sing.
sing, and sing, and sing, I soft - - ly sing, sing.
sing, and sing, and sing, I soft - - ly sing, sing.
sing, and sing, and sing, I soft - ly sing, sing.
mp p

90
G
f
I brood not o'er the bro-ken past, Nor dread
I brood not o'er the bro-ken past, Nor dread
I brood not o'er the past, o'er the bro - ken past, Nor
O'er the bro-ken past, Nor
G
f
96
mf
what - ev - er time may bring; No nights are
what - ev - er time may bring: No nights are
dread what - ev - er time may bring: No nights are
dread what - ev - er time may bring: No
mf

101
mp
mf
dark, no days are long, While
dark, no days are long, While
dark, no days are long, no days are long, While
nights are dark, no days are long, While
106
f
mf
in my heart, in my heart there swells a song, a song,
in my heart, in my heart there swells a song, a song,
in my heart, in my heart there swells a song, a song,
in my heart there swells a song, there swells a

111
p
mp
And I can sing, sing, sing, and I can sing, I can sing, I
And I can sing, sing, and I can sing, I can sing, I
And I can sing, sing, sing, and I can sing, I can sing, I
song, And I can sing, sing, and I can sing, I
116
cresc. poco a poco
ritardando
f
can sing, I can sing I can sing, sing.
can sing, I can sing, I can sing, sing, sing.
can sing, I can sing, I can sing, sing, sing.
can sing, I can sing, I can sing, sing, sing.